the Babysitter's Survival Guide

Modern Publishing
A Division of Unisystems, Inc.
New York, New York 10022
Printed in the U.S.A
Series UPC: 65065

Are You Ready?

So, you want to be a babysitter! Are you up to the challenge?
Take this quiz to find out where
you fit in and what to do next!

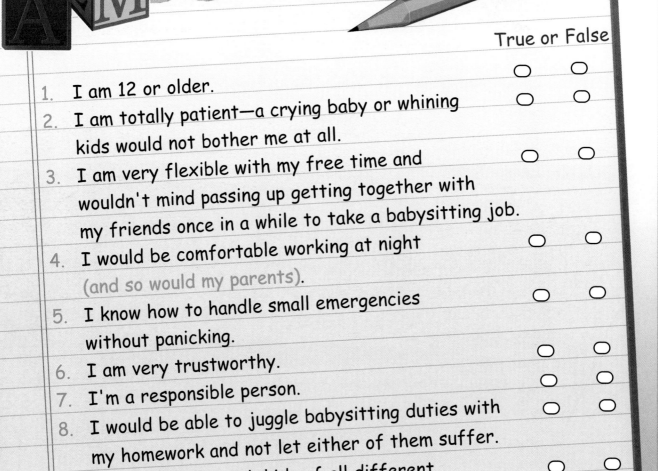

True or False

1. I am 12 or older. ◯ ◯
2. I am totally patient—a crying baby or whining ◯ ◯
   kids would not bother me at all.
3. I am very flexible with my free time and ◯ ◯
   wouldn't mind passing up getting together with
   my friends once in a while to take a babysitting job.
4. I would be comfortable working at night ◯ ◯
   (and so would my parents).
5. I know how to handle small emergencies ◯ ◯
   without panicking.
6. I am very trustworthy. ◯ ◯
7. I'm a responsible person. ◯ ◯
8. I would be able to juggle babysitting duties with ◯ ◯
   my homework and not let either of them suffer.
9. I enjoy playing with kids of all different ◯ ◯
   ages—even little babies!
10. I am very safety-conscious and not at all reckless. ◯ ◯

If you answered TRUE for:

8-10
You're totally ready for the responsibility of babysitting!

NEXT STEP: Sit down and talk to your parents and let them know that you'd like to start babysitting. Make sure that they're OK with your decision. Then, get the word out that you're starting up your babysitting career and have fun!

NEXT STEP: Sit down with your parents and go over the things that you need to work on. Talk about what you can do to get those skills up to speed.

5-7
You need to work on a couple of things before you get started. You're almost there!

4 or Less
Babysitting seems like fun—but it's hard work! You need to work on your skills.

NEXT STEP: Talk to your friends or other people that you know who babysit to get a really clear picture of what babysitting's all about. You'll realize exactly why you have to be a totally responsible person before you start caring for kids.

ARE YOU OLD ENOUGH?

Wondering if you're old enough to babysit?
What exactly is the right age, anyway?

There isn't one correct answer to those questions. It depends on a lot of things—where you live, who you will be babysitting for, etc. Most parents agree that they really don't want anyone younger than 12 to be in charge of the care of their kids!

There are a few good ways to find out if you're the right age. The first thing you should do is check with YOUR parents. Do they think that you are old enough? Then, check with your local employment agencies to see if there are any laws about legal ages of babysitters where you live. Also, check with your school or with local community centers (or online) to see if they have any age guidelines that they suggest.

Starting Out

OK—you've talked to your parents and they have agreed to let you launch your babysitting career! You've thought long and hard about it, have talked to different people about their babysitting experiences—you've even watched your younger siblings while your parents were home, as a test run!

But, where do you start? The best way to find babysitting work is by good old word-of-mouth. Your parents can let their friends and co-workers know that you want to start babysitting (after all, who wouldn't trust a parent's stamp of approval?). Tell your friends that you would be willing to fill in for them on their regular gigs if they can't make it.

Be patient. The first job is always the hardest to find. But, once you land your first job and do it well, your experience will speak for itself. Other jobs will start rolling in!

GETTING PAID
(IT IS A JOB AFTER ALL!)

You need to know ahead of time what you will charge for your wonderful babysitting services! Most parents are going to ask you what you charge.

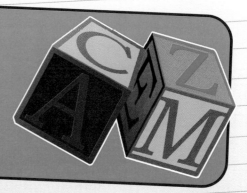

There's no set fee. You should find out what babysitters normally get paid in your area. This rate will vary from neighborhood to neighborhood. Ask your friends what they get paid and your parents can ask their friends who hire babysitters what they normally pay.

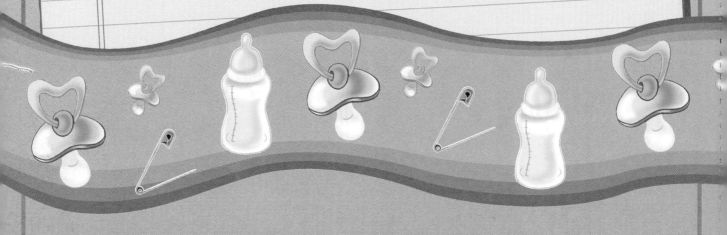

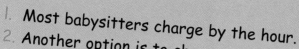

There are different ways to charge your clients:

1. Most babysitters charge by the hour.
2. Another option is to charge a flat fee (a set amount for the whole night).
3. You could charge on a price scale—a flat fee for a set number of hours, plus an additional amount per every hour after that.
4. Some babysitters charge per child (a certain dollar amount per hour, plus an additional $1 for each additional child).

Of course, if this is your first job, you shouldn't expect to get paid the same rate as someone with lots of experience. Once you have a good number of babysitting jobs under your belt and can offer good references, you will be able to charge more. Eventually, you will be able to charge the full rate for babysitters in your area.

Be sure to let the family you are babysitting for know how you would like to get paid, as well (in cash at the end of the night, run a tab that they can pay at the end of each month, etc.).

Ice-Breakers

You should definitely set up a pre-babysitting interview session with the parents and family. Here are some good questions to ask:

1. Are there any specific household rules?
2. How should I handle the kids if they misbehave?
3. Do the kids have homework they should be doing?
4. Are there any chores the kids have to do?
5. Do you have any pets? (If they do, you should meet them so that they get familiar with you.)
6. What are your kids' favorite activities?
7. Are there any areas of the house that are off-limits?
8. What are the kids' bedtime routines?
9. May I use the TV, radio or computer?
10. May I use the phone to make a short call?
11. How should I handle taking phone messages?

You should ask the parents to take you on a tour of the home so that you get familiar with it.

You should also ask to meet the kids, if you don't already know them, before you babysit!

IMPORTANT INFORMATION

Before you go on duty, sit down with the parents and fill out this information sheet together (front and back). If you become totally in-demand and need more checklists, jot down the info on a separate piece of paper for each new family (or photocopy this sheet while it's still blank).

FAMILY'S ADDRESS:_____
_____
_____
_____

PHONE NUMBER:_____

DOCTOR'S INFO

Name:
_____

Phone Number:
_____

WHERE PARENTS CAN BE REACHED:

Location:_____
Phone Number:_____
Time Parents Will Get Home:_____

EMERGENCY CONTACTS (IF PARENTS CAN'T BE REACHED):

1. **Name:**_____
   Phone Number:_____
2. **Name:**_____
   Phone Number:_____
3. **Name:**_____
   Phone Number:_____

NEAREST CROSS STREET:_____
_____
_____

NATIONAL POISON
CONTROL CENTER
HOTLINE: 1-800-222-1222

LOCAL FIRE DEPARTMENT
PHONE NUMBER:
_____

LOCAL POLICE
DEPARTMENT PHONE
NUMBER:
_____

IN CASE OF A MAJOR
EMERGENCY, DIAL 911!

CHILDREN'S INFO:

1. Name_____ Age:_____ Birthday:_____
2. Name_____ Age:_____ Birthday:_____
3. Name_____ Age:_____ Birthday:_____
4. Name_____ Age:_____ Birthday:_____

MEDICAL CONDITIONS OR ALLERGIES TO BE NOTED:
_____
_____
_____

FAMILY DO'S AND DON'TS

Foods Child/Children **CAN** Eat:

BEDTIME(S):
_____
_____
_____

Foods Child/Children **CANNOT** Eat:

TV Shows/Channels Child/Children Are Allowed to Watch:

TV Shows/Channels Child/Children Are **NOT** Allowed to Watch:

Other Things Child/Children are **NOT** Allowed To Do:

Safety First

The most important part of your job is to keep the kids (and yourself) safe and sound. After all, that's why the parents hired you! In order to do that, sit down with the parents and go over this safety questionnaire before your start babysitting.

- Do you have an emergency phone numbers list updated and near a telephone?
- Where are your smoke detectors and fire extinguishers located?
- Where do you keep your first aid kit?
- What is your family fire escape plan?
- What is your policy on the children using the internet?
- Where is the fuse box located?
- Where do you keep flashlights?
- Where is your evacuation location?
- Are the children allergic to anything that I should know about ahead of time?

WHEN TO CALL 911

🌼 911 should only be called in cases of very serious emergencies—this means to report a fire, a crime that is being committed, a break-in, a very serious accident or any situation where someone is in danger of being seriously hurt or killed. In any other case, call one of your emergency contact numbers instead of calling 911.

A REAL LIFESAVER
It would be a really great idea for you to learn CPR. It's a life-saving technique and you never know when you might need it! Go online or check with your school to see where you can find CPR certification classes.

It's important to know what to do when you call 911:

1. Stay calm. Know the address and phone number of where you are. Give your cell phone number, if you have one.

2. Be ready to tell the dispatcher what kind of emergency you are calling to report.

3. If you are reporting an injury, be ready to describe exactly what is wrong with the victim.

4. Be ready to give the victim's age and weight.

5. Do not hang up unless the dispatcher tells you to do so.

Safety ✓ Checklist

Run down this safety checklist. You should always be prepared!

- It's best to stay away from all kitchen appliances. But, if the parents ask you to make a meal, be sure that you know how to use all of the appliances ahead of time.

- Be sure that all windows and doors are securely locked.

- If the house has a security alarm, make sure that you ask the parents to show you how to use it.

- If a smoke detector goes off, NEVER assume that it has gone off accidentally. Check out the house for smoke or flames.

- Never leave kids alone outside and NEVER EVER let them go near a street unattended (of course, that's IF you have the parents' permission to take the kids outside).

- Be sure that you know what the kids can and cannot eat. If you are feeding a small child, make sure to cut the food into small pieces to avoid choking.

- Do not let the kids near any water that they can drown in—this means tubs, toilets, pools, even something as small as a bucket of water. In fact, keep the bathroom door closed at all times!

- Keep all medicines out of the kids' reach.

- Don't let the kids climb on tables, counters, ladders, etc.

- Avoid burns by keeping the kids away from ovens, stoves, hot water, lighters, matches, etc.

- Keep cleaning products and anything else that is poisonous out of the reach of children.

- Do not let the kids play with or near any sharp objects.

- Do not let the kids play with anything small enough that they could choke on.

- Keep cords, rope, string, ribbons or anything that kids could wrap around their necks away from them.

- Never answer the door unless the parents tell you to do so.

- Never tell anyone that you are alone in the house with the kids.

- The best rule of thumb is to make sure the kids are in your sight at ALL times. While they are sleeping, peek in and check on them every twenty minutes or so.

BABYSITTER BASICS!

There are some basics that every babysitter should know before they go into business! Check out these do's and don'ts before you take on your next job.

1. Arrive a few minutes early—you don't want to keep the parents waiting if they have somewhere to go!

2. Be sure to ask the parents any questions you may have before they leave. You should only call them on their cell phones while they are out if there's an emergency or something unexpected comes up.

3. Follow any routines that the parents set up for you. These are most likely the routines that make the kids most comfortable.

4. Interact with the kids. If you're playing with them, they are less likely to get hurt or into trouble.

5. Don't invite visitors over. It's not very professional!

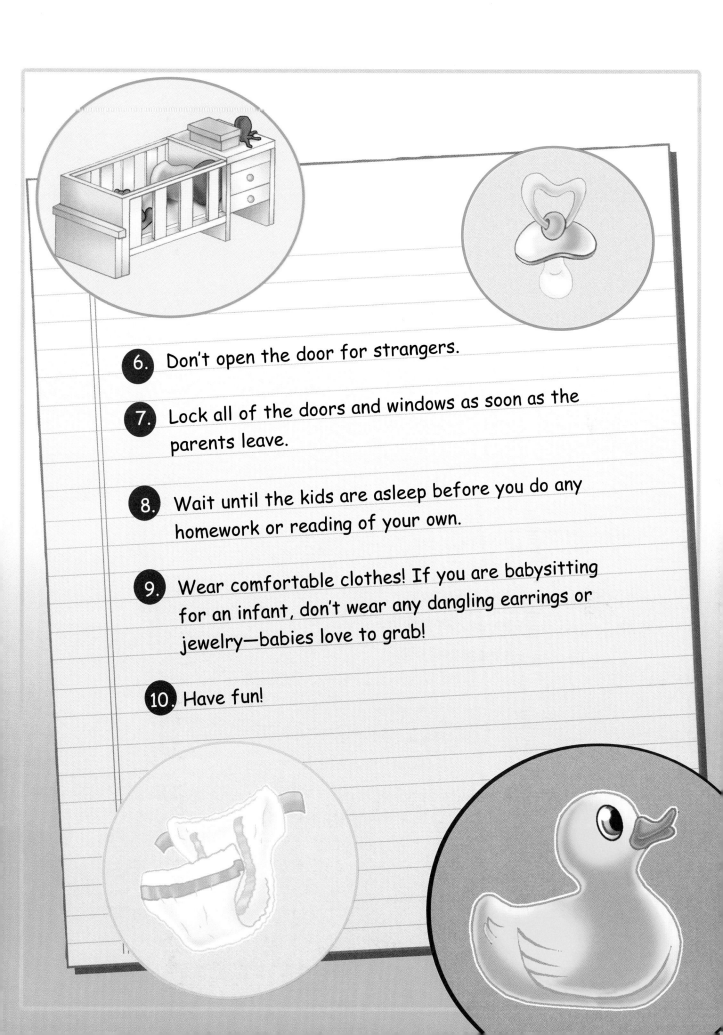

6. Don't open the door for strangers.

7. Lock all of the doors and windows as soon as the parents leave.

8. Wait until the kids are asleep before you do any homework or reading of your own.

9. Wear comfortable clothes! If you are babysitting for an infant, don't wear any dangling earrings or jewelry—babies love to grab!

10. Have fun!

Tips of the Trade!

Do you want to become known as THE best babysitter in your neighborhood? Well, then you have to go above and beyond and add those special touches!

Keep the house neat and tidy! The last thing parents want to do is come home and have to clean up after their kids—and you!

Be positive! Try not to complain or say negative things to the parents when they get home.

Honesty is the best policy! Never lie. If something breaks, don't hide it. If you didn't do something that the parents asked you to, let them know. They'll appreciate that more than a cover-up.

Give the parents a full report. Let them know what you and the kids did, if everyone did their homework, if someone didn't eat, if someone got a bump or a bruise—anything that you think is important.

Ask for another gig! Let them know that you are available to babysit for them again!

Parents are going to want to know all about the person who will be in charge of the care of their kids. So, every time you babysit for a new family, fill out one of these info sheets (front and back) and give it to the parents. Jot down the info on a blank sheet of paper or make photocopies so that you have enough.

MY BABYSITTING REPORT

MY NAME: _____

AGE: _____

HOME PHONE NUMBER:
_____

CELL PHONE NUMBER:
_____

ADDRESS: _____
_____
_____

PARENTS' NAMES:_____

PARENTS' CELL PHONE NUMBERS:
_____
_____

PARENTS' WORK PHONE NUMBERS:
_____
_____

MEDICAL INFO OR ALLERGIES TO BE NOTED:
_____
_____
_____

REFERENCES:
_____
_____
_____

ADDITIONAL INFO:
_____
_____
_____
_____

Notes:

MY BABYSITTING Background

NUMBER OF BABYSITTING
JOBS I'VE HAD:

___ 1
___ 2-5
___ 6-9
___ More Than 10

THE MOST CHILDREN I'VE
WATCHED AT ONE TIME:

___ 1
___ 2
___ 3
___ 4 or More

THE YOUNGEST CHILD I'VE
CARED FOR:

___ Infant (up to 12 months old)
___ 1 to 3 Years Old
___ 4 to 5 Years Old
___ 6 Years Old or Older

THE LONGEST BABYSITTING
JOB I EVER HAD:

___ 1 Hour
___ 2 to 3 Hours
___ 4 to 5 Hours
___ 6 Hours or More

MY PARENTS ALLOW ME TO ACCEPT
BABYSITTING JOBS
(check all that apply):

___ On Weekdays
___ On Weekend Nights
___ On Weeknights
___ During the School Year
___ On Weekend Days
___ During Vacation from School

MY PARENTS WILL NOT ALLOW ME TO
ACCEPT THESE KINDS OF JOBS:

_____
_____
_____
_____
_____

HOW I PREFER TO GET TO
AND FROM JOBS:

___ On My Own
___ A Ride from My Parents
___ A Ride from the Children's Parents

I AM NOT ALLOWED TO BABYSIT PAST:

___ 10 PM
___ 11 PM
___ Midnight
___ Other

Kid Kit

Babysitting isn't as simple as showing up and making sure the kids don't get into trouble! The best (and most well-liked) babysitters are the ones who interact with the kids! Most times, the homes you babysit in will be stocked with the kids' toys and games. But, just to be on the safe side, pack your own Babysitter's Kit!
Here's a great list of things to pack:

- A First-Aid Kit (some bandages and antiseptic ointment)
- Coloring Books
- Crayons
- Books to Read
- A Board Game or Two
- Playing Cards
- Flash Cards
- Video Games
- DVDs (kid-appropriate, of course!)
- CDs (again, nothing too mature for the little ones)
- Puzzles
- Stickers
- Dolls
- Toy Cars
- Blocks

Remember to personalize the kit for the family you are babysitting for on a given night! Are you sitting for girls or boys? Infants, toddlers or older kids?

BOREDOM BUSTERS!

Don't just plop the kids in front of the TV and do your homework! Play with the kids and have a great time! You'll have fun, they'll have a blast and stay out of trouble—and, the bonus is that you'll tire them out and make bedtime a breeze! Don't know what to play?
Here are some great ideas!

Play Peek-A-Boo!

It sounds too simple, but babies (newborn to 1 year old) love it! Just hold your hands over your face, then pull them away and say "Peek-a-boo!" The baby will want you to do it over and over again!

Scavenger Hunt!

Make a list of ten things that the kids can find around the house (make sure that these things are really in the house somewhere—you don't want the kids to get frustrated). Then give each kid a list of what they need to find. The first person to find all ten things wins! (If the kids are very young, make sure you walk around the house with them while they are hunting!)

Play a board game or cards!

Read to the kids!

Color with the kids!

Fashion Show!
Put on a fashion show! Have the kids dress up in their most fun clothes and walk the runway!

Tea Party!
Have a pretend tea party and have the little girl invite all of her dolls and teddy bears!

Story Time!
Make up a fun story to tell the kids. Then have the kids make up stories to tell you! Or, you can start a story, and then have each person take turns making up the next part!

TALES

Sing-A-Long!

Put on the radio and sing and dance! Kids have lots of energy, and dancing is a great way to put that energy to use! Another fun musical thing to do is make up silly lyrics to songs!

Old Standards!
If all else fails, play pretend school, pretend restaurant or pretend store! These are old favorites that kids are sure to love!

Make a Tent!
This one's easy! Just grab a sheet or a blanket and drape it over two pieces of furniture that are right next to each other. Then, get under it, and pretend that you are camping!

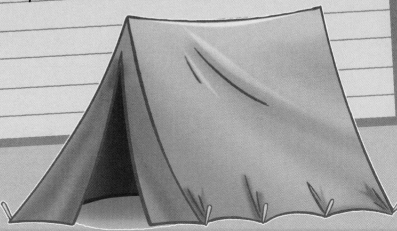

Play Simon Says!

Choose one of the kids to be Simon. Simon tells the other kids to do things like touch their nose or stand on one foot, saying "Simon says" before each instruction. Every once in a while, Simon will give an instruction without saying "Simon says" first. If any of the other kids perform that action, they are out of the game. The last person in wins!

Crafts For Kids!

If you've tried everything and the kids are still restless and bored, try making any of these fun and easy crafts:

Paper Hats
Fold fun and silly paper hats out of newspaper. Then have the kids color them!

Collages!

Find old magazines and newspapers. Cut out pictures (make sure you are the one handling the scissors, unless they are safe children's scissors) of the child's favorite things. Glue or tape the pictures all over a piece of construction paper.

Troubleshooting

Sometimes, no matter what you do, you just can't seem to make a kid happy or stop him or her from being fussy. Here are some reasons why kids might be in a bad mood and what you should do when kids misbehave.

FUSS-O-METER

Run down this checklist when the kids you are sitting for just won't stop whining:

Is the kid bored? Try a fun game or a toy.
Is the kid hungry? Try a snack—it might do the trick.
Is the kid tired? Is it past bedtime or time for a nap?

MISBEHAVING 101

Here are some tips on how to handle the
kids when they misbehave:

- Take the kid into a different room or try a different toy. Sometimes changing the situation helps.

- Make sure you're firm (but kind) and don't let the kids push you around. You are in charge and the kids should know it.

- Be clear about the rules. Let the kids know what you will and will not accept from them. A time-out might do the trick. Let a child off by having him or her sitting alone for a few minutes.

- Be fair and don't favor one child over the other.

- If siblings fight a lot, separate them.

- If it's OK with the parents (clear this ahead of time), let the kids know that bad behavior will result in discipline. Take away a favorite toy or game.

NEVER, NEVER, NEVER hit a child or use abusive or bad language! This is never acceptable, under any circumstances!

Notes and Stuff

Jot down all of your notes here! Whether it's something important about a particular family, a great tip you learned, or an awesome babysitting website that you found, you won't want to forget it!

My Busy Schedule

DAY: _____
DATE: _____
BABYSITTING FOR: _____
TIME: _____

DAY: _____
DATE: _____
BABYSITTING FOR: _____
TIME: _____

DAY: _____
DATE: _____
BABYSITTING FOR: _____
TIME: _____

DAY: _____
DATE: _____
BABYSITTING FOR: _____
TIME: _____

DAY: _____
DATE: _____
BABYSITTING FOR: _____
TIME: _____

My Busy Schedule

DAY: _____
DATE: _____
BABYSITTING FOR: _____
TIME: _____

DAY: _____
DATE: _____
BABYSITTING FOR: _____
TIME: _____

DAY: _____
DATE: _____
BABYSITTING FOR: _____
TIME: _____

DAY: _____
DATE: _____
BABYSITTING FOR: _____
TIME: _____

DAY: _____
DATE: _____
BABYSITTING FOR: _____
TIME: _____

BEDTIME BASICS!

Getting the kids to go to sleep
"without a fuss" can be a real challenge!
Be prepared!

TIME

The first rule of thumb is to stick to the bedtimes set. Of course, playtime might run a little long or it might have taken a few extra minutes to clean up after dinner, so pushing bedtime off by a few minutes sometimes happens! But don't let the kids talk you into letting them stay up much later than their bedtime!

PREPARATION

Bedtime isn't as easy as putting the kids into bed and closing the door! Keep in mind that the pre-bedtime routine—washing hands and faces, brushing teeth, putting on pajamas, etc.—can take between 30 and 45 minutes! Make sure you start at an early enough time.

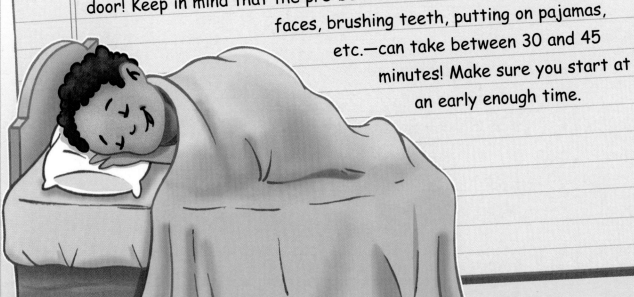

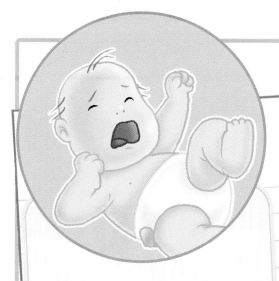

If the kids just won't go to sleep, try some of these great tips!

Sing a nice, calming song or lullaby!

If you're babysitting for an infant, rock the baby! (REMEMBER: Always lay a baby on his or her back to go to sleep—never on the stomach!)

Promise that you'll check on the child—this is reassuring. And, if you promise to check, make sure you do it, even if you think the child is asleep!

WARNING

Most kids don't want playtime to end and bedtime to begin! So, it's not a very good idea to announce that it's bedtime two minutes before it's time to hit the sack. About 15 minutes before their scheduled bedtime, let the kids know. This way, they have time to finish up playtime and will move easily from one activity to the next—bedtime!

STORYTIME

Reading a story together is a great way to end the day and help the kids relax and get ready to sleep. Pick a fun storybook, and, when the child is snuggled up in bed, read the story!

SCARED OF THE DARK

Find out from the parents if the child is scared of the dark—that's very common! If so, be sure to leave the hall light on with the door cracked, or plug in a nightlight.

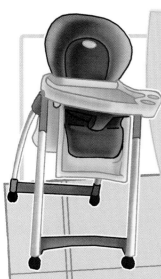

Let's Eat

Odds are, the kids WILL get hungry while you are
babysitting—either for a meal or for a snack.
Here are some mealtime tips!

First of all, check with the parents to find out
what they want you to feed the kids and at what time.

- Make sure that food is cut into small enough pieces for the
kids—nothing too big that they could choke on.

- If you are babysitting for an infant and you are preparing a bottle,
make sure that the milk or formula is not too hot. Sprinkle a couple
of drops on your wrist. If it's too hot for you, then it's too hot for
the baby.

- Make sure any food you prepare for the kids is not too hot.

- If you are having a meal, it's best to sit down at the kitchen or
dining room table.

- Help younger kids cut their food—never give them any sharp utensils
to use by themselves!

- Use sturdy plastic cups—never glass, which can easily break!

- Don't ever leave the kids unattended while they are eating.

- Clean up! Wash any dishes or utensils that you use.
Never leave a mess!

BABYSITTING RECAP

Give the parents a recap of what went on while they were gone! Photocopy these checklists so that you don't run out!

What We Did!

The Kids Ate _____

The Kids Went to Bed at _____

We Played _____

We Read _____

We Watched _____

Phone Messages _____

Notes

What We Did!

The Kids Ate _____

The Kids Went to Bed at _____

We Played _____

We Read _____

We Watched _____

Phone Messages _____

Notes

BABYSITTING RECAP

Give the parents a recap of what went on while they were gone! Photocopy these checklists so that you don't run out!

What We Did!

The Kids Ate _____

The Kids Went to Bed at _____

We Played _____

We Read _____

We Watched _____

Phone Messages _____

Notes

What We Did!

The Kids Ate _____

The Kids Went to Bed at _____

We Played _____

We Read _____

We Watched _____

Phone Messages _____

Notes

MISSING MOMMY AND DADDY

Don't be alarmed if the kid you are babysitting starts to cry when his or her parents leave! It's not you—it's totally normal for the kids (especially little ones) to miss their parents and be a little bit scared. Here's what to do:

- Reassure them to calm them down. Let them know that their parents will be back soon (but don't lie and tell them that they will be back earlier than they really will). It helps kids to know that their parents won't be gone forever!

- Give the child a hug.

- Be prepared to take their minds off the fact that their parents just left.

- Ask the child to show you his or her bedroom to distract them.

- Offer a treat like a cookie or a piece of candy.

- Ask to see the child's toys. This will likely lead to playing, which will end the crying.

- If you have tried EVERYTHING that you can possibly think of and the child has been crying for a very LONG time, it's best to call the parents. They might be able to offer a method that will work.

You're The Referee!

If you're babysitting for more than one kid at a time, especially if they're siblings, odds are they'll have an argument or two. It happens! Learn how to handle the situation like a pro!

The kids might be looking for attention. So, don't ignore the situation. Stop what you're doing and talk to the kids.

Be sure to pay close attention to **BOTH** sides of the argument. Be fair—don't take sides!

Make sure that the fighting doesn't get physical and that the kids don't hurt each other.

Give both kids time to cool off. Tell them to stand in opposite corners of the room or in different rooms.

Encourage the kids to talk out the problem. Sit them down and give each kid a couple of minutes to tell their side of the story. Come up with a compromise together.

If the kids can't agree on a compromise, YOU come up with one! After all, you are the one in charge.

If there's just no end to the argument in sight, take away the toy or game that's causing the fight. This way, no one wins. It may seem harsh, but that might be the only solution.

Nursery Rhymes

Little kids really love nursery rhymes! Here are some really popular rhymes. Read them to the kids. Here's a fun twist that will entertain the little ones—ask them to act out the rhymes!

Humpty-Dumpty

Humpty-Dumpty sat on a wall,
Humpty-Dumpty had a great fall,
All the King's horses and all the King's men,
Could not put Humpty-Dumpty together again.

Little Miss Muffet

Little Miss Muffet,
Sat on a tuffet,
Eating her curds and whey,
Along came a spider,
And sat down beside her,
And frightened Miss Muffet away.

This Little Piggy

This little piggy went to market.
This little piggy stayed home.
This little piggy had a bit of meat.
This little piggy had none.
And the last little piggy said,
"Oh, dear me! I can't find my way home."

Hey! Diddle, Diddle

Hey! Diddle, Diddle,
The cat and the fiddle,
The cow jumped over the moon.
The little dog laughed,
To see such a sport,
And the dish ran away with the spoon.

Hickory, Dickory, Dock

Hickory, dickory, dock,
The mouse ran up the clock,
The clock struck one,
The mouse ran down,
Hickory, dickory, dock.

GAME TIME!

Here are some fun games to play with the kids if everyone is bored!

HANGMAN

One player thinks of a word and draws dashes to represent the letters in that word under the hangman board. The other player tries to guess the word by guessing a letter at a time. Every time the player guesses a letter that is not in the secret word, the other player draws a part of the hangman. If the player guesses a letter that is in the secret word, it gets filled in. If the player guesses the word before ALL of the parts of the hangman are drawn (a head, a body, two legs, two arms), he or she wins. If the hangman is fully drawn before the word is guessed, the guessing player loses!

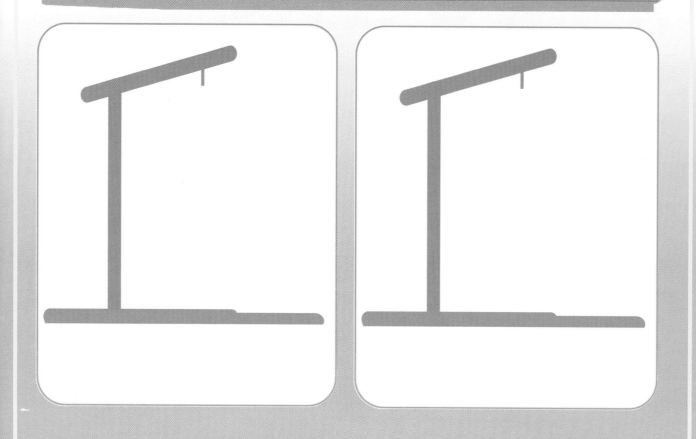

DOTS

This games needs two players. Each player takes a turn drawing a straight line from one dot to another. Any time the line you draw is the last line of a box (a complete box is formed after you draw your line), put your initial in that box. The player with the most initials on the board at the end of the game wins!

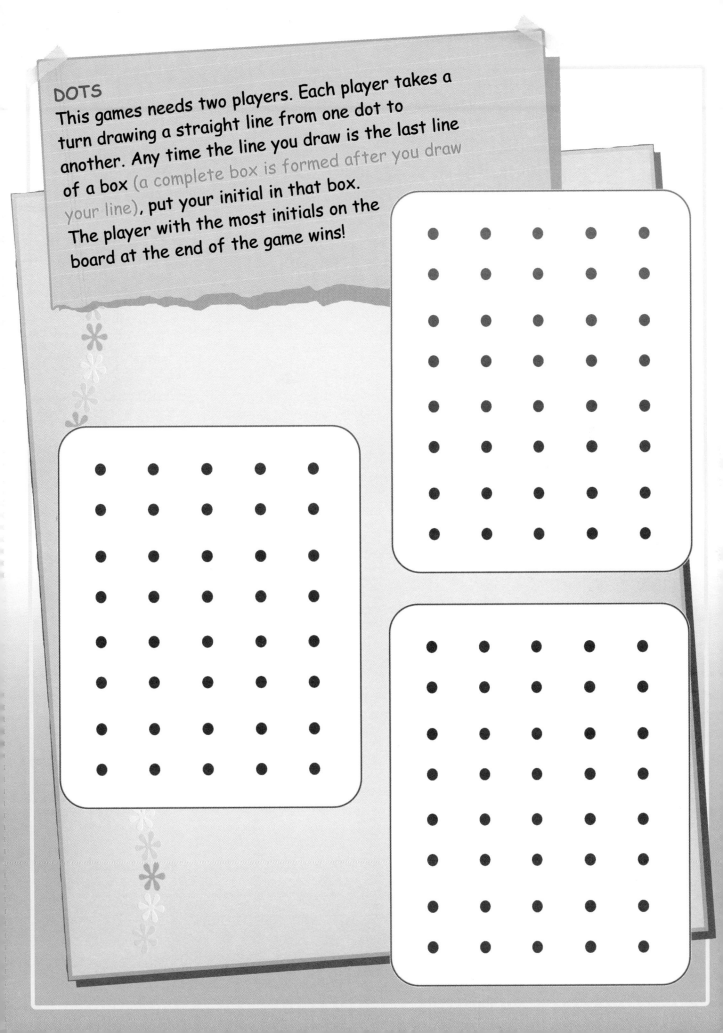

Some More Games!

Sometimes, kids get bored playing with the same toys or watching the same videos over and over again. Try tic-tac-toe! It's a great way to keep the kids occupied—for a little while!

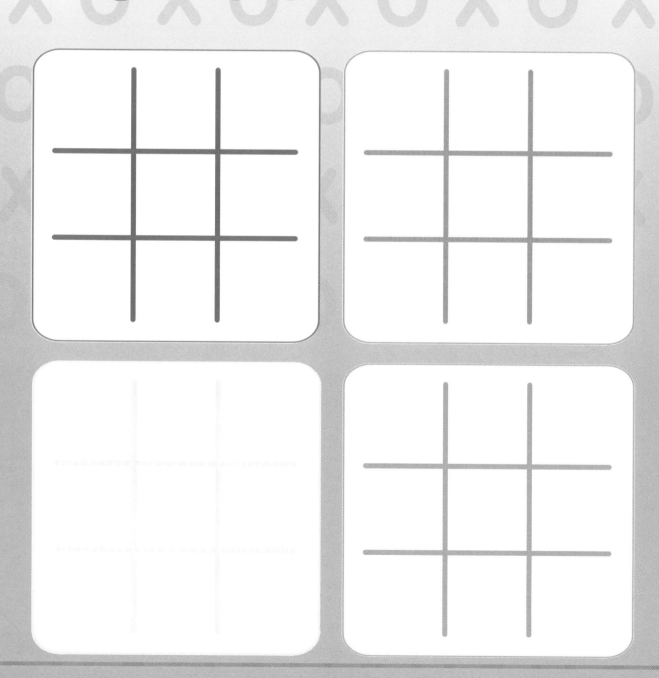

Stuff to Remember

Every family is different—and you don't want to mix up one kid's favorite song with another's! Here's a great way to keep track of your clients!

FAMILY:

KIDS' NAMES:

NOTES:

FAMILY:

KIDS' NAMES:

NOTES:

FAMILY:

KIDS' NAMES:

NOTES:

FAMILY:

KIDS' NAMES:

NOTES:

Now that you're a top-of-the-line babysitter and you have a few regular clients, why not spread the word about your awesome babysitting services? Fill out these business cards and have your regulars (and your family and friends) pass them out to people that they know who need a wonderful babysitter!

World's Best Babysitter!

References Available!

Name:
Phone Number:
Email Address:

World's Best Babysitter!

References Available!

Name:
Phone Number:
Email Address:

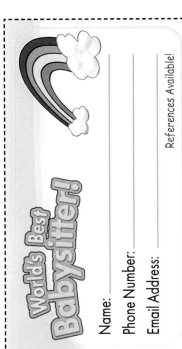

World's Best Babysitter!

References Available!

Name:
Phone Number:
Email Address:

World's Best Babysitter!

References Available!

Name:
Phone Number:
Email Address:

World's Best Babysitter!

References Available!

Name:
Phone Number:
Email Address:

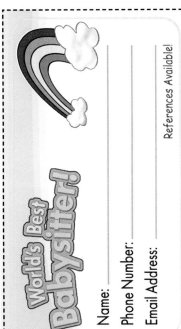

World's Best Babysitter!

References Available!

Name:
Phone Number:
Email Address:

BABYSITTER FOR HIRE!

BABYSITTER FOR HIRE!

BABYSITTER FOR HIRE!

BABYSITTER FOR HIRE!

BABYSITTER FOR HIRE!

BABYSITTER FOR HIRE!